Boublil and Schönberg's

THE PIRATE QUEEN

RIVERDREAM
UNDER THE DIRECTION OF
MOYA DOHERTY   JOHN McCOLGAN
PRESENTS
BOUBLIL & SCHÖNBERG'S

A NEW MUSICAL

BOOK BY
ALAIN BOUBLIL   CLAUDE-MICHEL SCHÖNBERG
and RICHARD MALTBY, JR.

MUSIC BY
CLAUDE-MICHEL SCHÖNBERG

LYRICS BY
ALAIN BOUBLIL   RICHARD MALTBY, JR.   JOHN DEMPSEY

BASED UPON THE NOVEL, "GRANIA – SHE KING OF THE IRISH SEAS" BY MORGAN LLYWELYN

STARRING
Stephanie J. Block   Hadley Fraser
Linda Balgord   Marcus Chait   Jeff McCarthy   William Youmans

WITH
Nick Adams, Richard Todd Adams, Caitlin Allen, Sean Beglan, Timothy W. Bish, Jerad Bortz, Troy Edward Bowles,
Grady McLeod Bowman, Rachel Bress, Don Brewer, Kimilee Bryant, Alexis Ann Carra, Noelle Curran, Bobbie Ann Dunn,
Brooke Elliott, Justin Fernandez, Christopher Garbrecht, Eric Hatch, Cristin J. Hubbard, David Koch, Timothy Kochka, Jamie LaVerdiere,
Joseph Mahowald, Tokiko Masuda, Christopher Grey Misa, Padraic Moyles, Brian O'Brien, Kyle James O'Connor, Michael James Scott,
Greg Stone, Katie Erin Tomlinson, Daniel Torres, Áine Uí Cheallaigh, Kathy Voytko, Jennifer Waiser, Briana Yacavone

SCENIC DESIGN	COSTUME DESIGN	LIGHTING DESIGN	SOUND DESIGN
EUGENE LEE	MARTIN PAKLEDINAZ	KENNETH POSNER	JONATHAN DEANS
HAIR DESIGN	SPECIAL EFFECTS DESIGN	AERIAL SEQUENCE DESIGN	MAKE-UP DESIGN
PAUL HUNTLEY	GREGORY MEEH	PAUL RUBIN	ANGELINA AVALLONE
SCENIC DESIGN ASSOCIATE	FIGHT DIRECTOR	ASSOCIATE DIRECTOR	ASSOCIATE CHOREOGRAPHER
EDWARD PIERCE	J. STEVEN WHITE	TARA YOUNG	RACHEL BRESS
CASTING	PRODUCTION MANAGER	PRODUCTION STAGE MANAGER	MUSICAL COORDINATOR
TARA RUBIN CASTING	PETER W. LAMB	C. RANDALL WHITE	MSI/SAM LUTFIYYA

MARKETING	GENERAL PRESS REPRESENTATIVE	ASSOCIATE PRODUCER
TMG-THE MARKETING GROUP	BONEAU BRYAN-BROWN	DANCAP PRODUCTIONS, INC.
EXECUTIVE PRODUCER (DEVELOPMENT)	EXECUTIVE PRODUCER	GENERAL MANAGEMENT
RONAN SMITH	EDGAR DOBIE	THEATRE PRODUCTION GROUP LLC
ORCHESTRATIONS, VOCAL ARRANGEMENTS, MUSICAL SUPERVISION & DIRECTION	ARTISTIC DIRECTOR	IRISH DANCE CHOREOGRAPHER
JULIAN KELLY	JOHN McCOLGAN	CAROL LEAVY JOYCE

MUSICAL STAGING
GRACIELA DANIELE

DIRECTED BY
FRANK GALATI

Photos courtesy of Joan Marcus and Boneau/Bryan-Brown

ISBN-13: 978-1-4234-2987-6
ISBN-10: 1-4234-2987-7

BOUBERG MUSIC LIMITED

EXCLUSIVELY DISTRIBUTED BY

7777 W. BLUEMOUND RD. P.O. BOX 13819 MILWAUKEE, WI 53213

Visit Hal Leonard Online at
www.halleonard.com

WOMAN

Music by CLAUDE-MICHEL SCHÖNBERG
Lyrics by ALAIN BOUBLIL, RICHARD MALTBY, JR.
and JOHN DEMPSEY

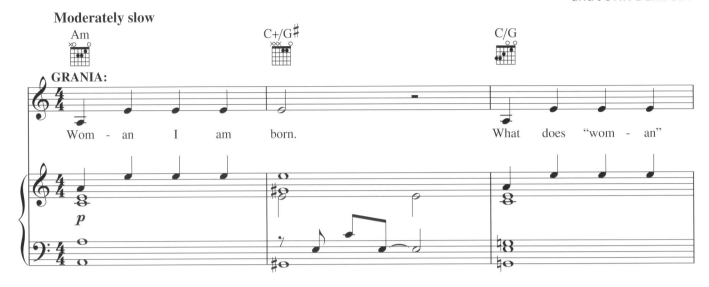

HERE ON THIS NIGHT

Music by CLAUDE-MICHEL SCHÖNBERG
Lyrics by ALAIN BOUBLIL, RICHARD MALTBY, JR.
and JOHN DEMPSEY

TIERNAN:

I went to sea when I was ten.

I'd sail the world for months or more. I would be leagues a-way, but

then I'd dream of you back on the shore.

Now that you'll al-ways be in sight, my life be-gins here on this

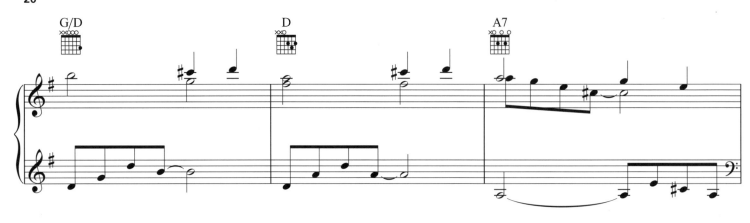

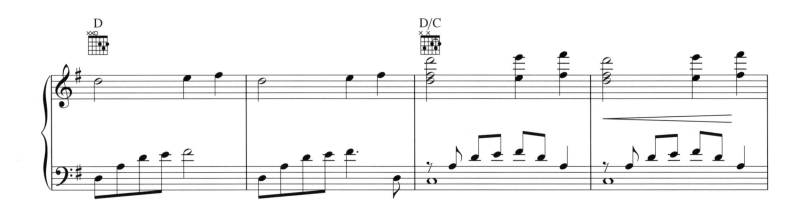

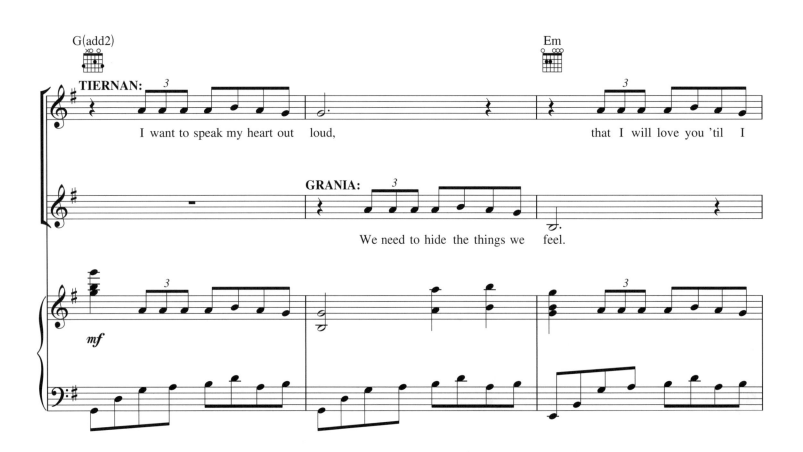

TIERNAN: I want to speak my heart out loud, that I will love you 'til I

GRANIA: We need to hide the things we feel.

BOYS'LL BE BOYS

Music by CLAUDE-MICHEL SCHÖNBERG
Lyrics by ALAIN BOUBLIL, RICHARD MALTBY, JR.
and JOHN DEMPSEY

Moderately fast, rowdy

THE WEDDING

Music by CLAUDE-MICHEL SCHÖNBERG
Lyrics by ALAIN BOUBLIL, RICHARD MALTBY, JR.
and JOHN DEMPSEY

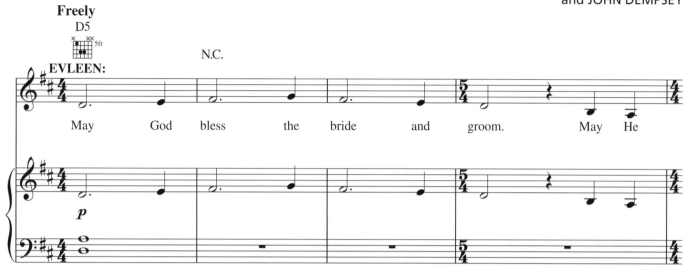

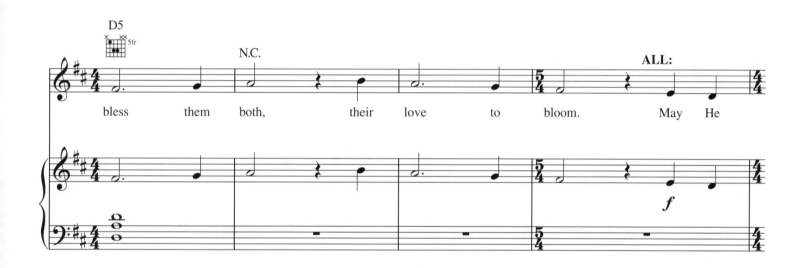

un - ion. May God bless the bride and

Lively

groom on this day._____

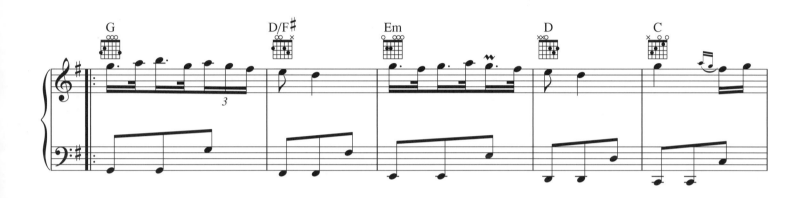

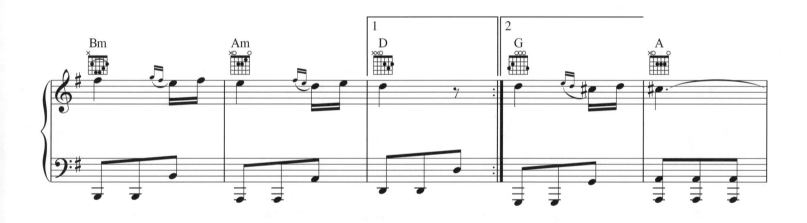

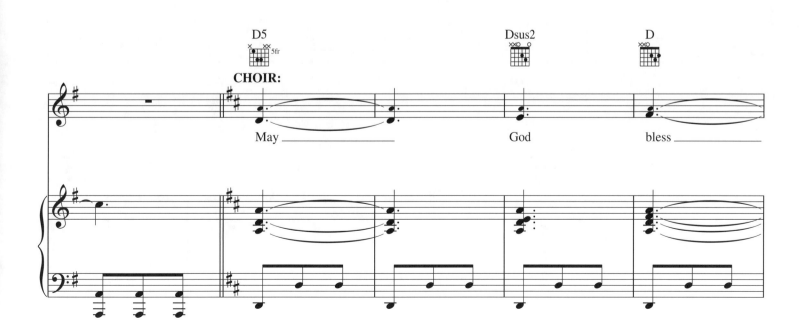

CHOIR:

May _____ God _____ bless _____

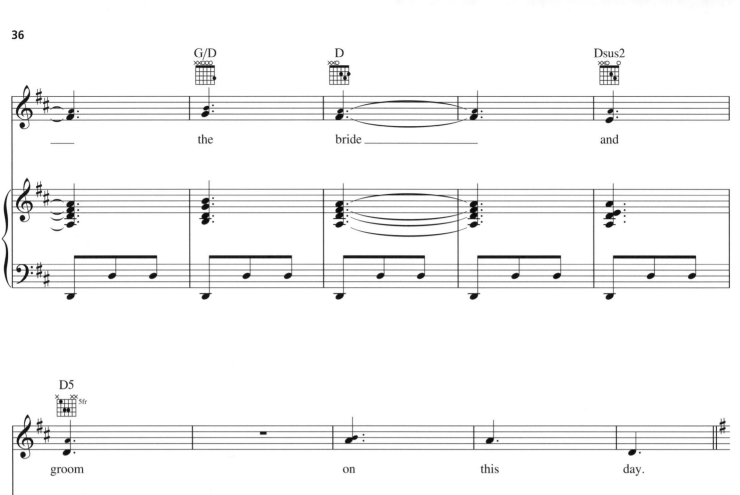

the bride and

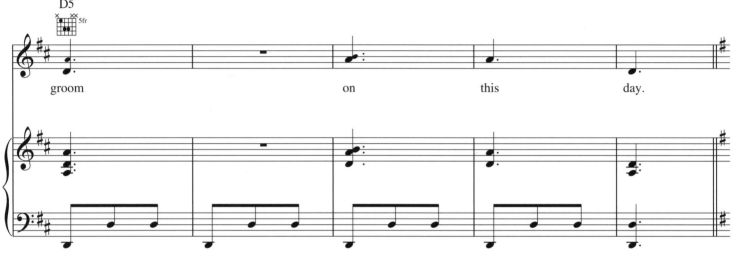

groom on this day.

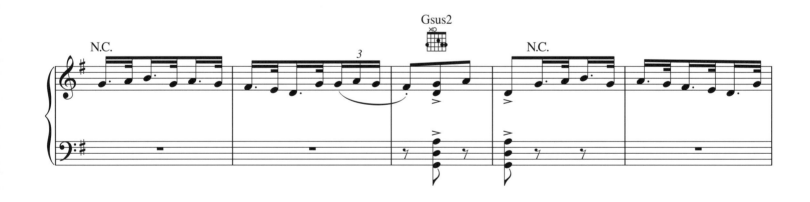

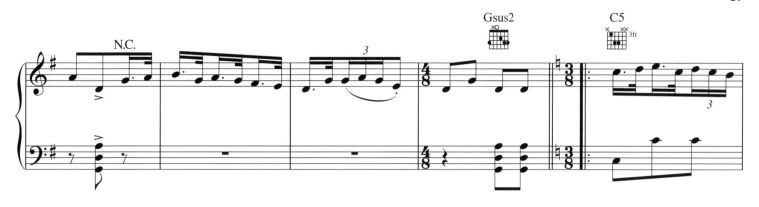

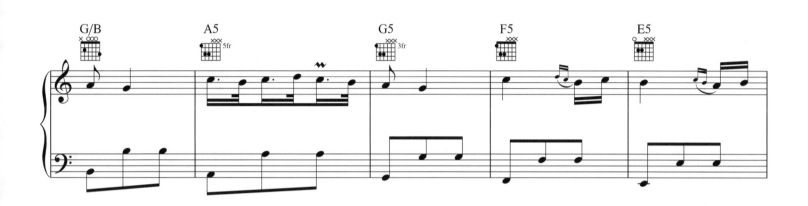

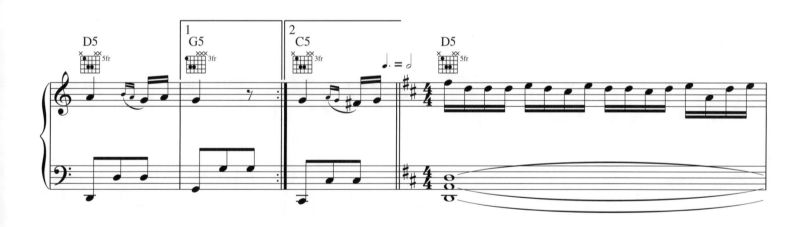

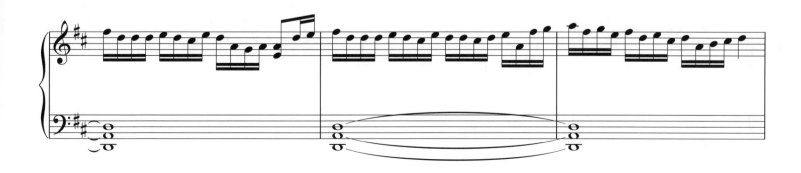

I'LL BE THERE

Music by CLAUDE-MICHEL SCHÖNBERG
Lyrics by ALAIN BOUBLIL, RICHARD MALTBY, JR.
and JOHN DEMPSEY

44

He'll keep his wife ___ dressed up in bows, ___ lav-ished e - ter-
- nal - ly ___ with flow'rs.
But what-ev - er life ___ he might pro - pose ___ will be mere - ly pre -
tend - ing to the dream nev - er end - ing

A Day Beyond Belclare

Music by CLAUDE-MICHEL SCHÖNBERG
Lyrics by ALAIN BOUBLIL, RICHARD MALTBY, JR.
and JOHN DEMPSEY

we'll bond _ on our way, _____

march - ing through _ the twelve bens _ and on _ to Clew Bay. _

ENSEMBLE:

mf *dim. poco a poco*

A day be - yond Bel -

clare, _____ your fa - ther waits for you. _____

SAIL TO THE STARS

Music by CLAUDE-MICHEL SCHÖNBERG
Lyrics by ALAIN BOUBLIL, RICHARD MALTBY, JR.
and JOHN DEMPSEY

I DISMISS YOU

Music by CLAUDE-MICHEL SCHÖNBERG
Lyrics by ALAIN BOUBLIL, RICHARD MALTBY, JR.
and JOHN DEMPSEY

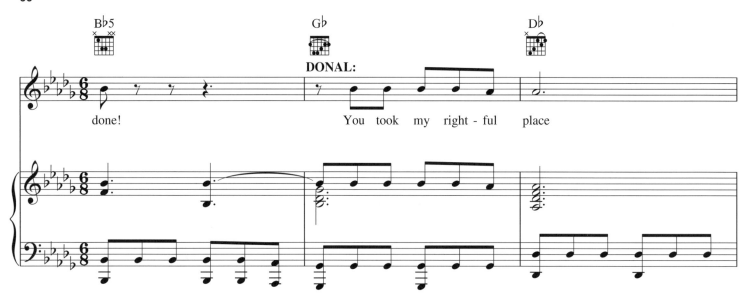

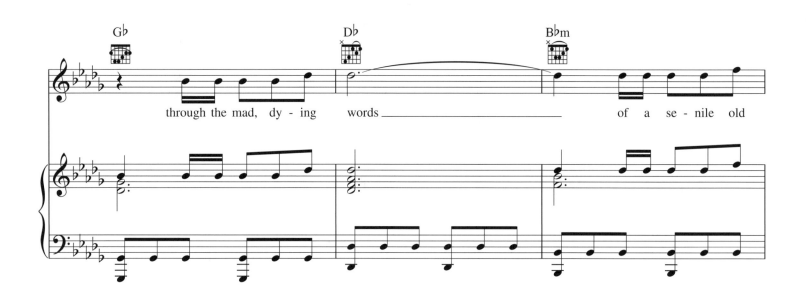

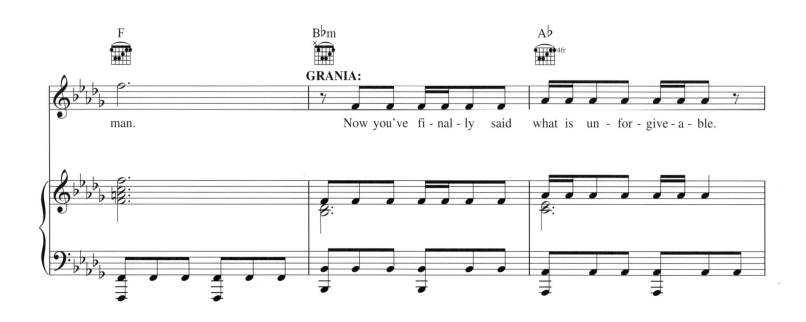

IF I SAID I LOVED YOU

Music by CLAUDE-MICHEL SCHÖNBERG
Lyrics by ALAIN BOUBLIL, RICHARD MALTBY, JR.
and JOHN DEMPSEY

THE ROLE OF THE QUEEN

Music by CLAUDE-MICHEL SCHÖNBERG
Lyrics by ALAIN BOUBLIL, RICHARD MALTBY, JR.
and JOHN DEMPSEY

THE SEA OF LIFE

Music by CLAUDE-MICHEL SCHÖNBERG
Lyrics by ALAIN BOUBLIL, RICHARD MALTBY, JR.
and JOHN DEMPSEY

GRANIA:
I'm at home ___ with the wind on my

SAILORS:
On ___ the sea ___ of life, ___

face. I've a place ___ as a wom-an up-on the

what ___ can be, ___ will be. ___

sea, Shel - tered in ___ the brine's ___ em-brace,

and this mo - ment ___ in time con - stant is ___ the